Introduction

In a time when things seem rather despairing and when the news of the day often seems to be nothing other than bad news, what hope is there? Today there are people dying with no hope and, perhaps even worse, people living without hope.

Yet such a seemingly dark and gloomy outlook is not the be all and end all: there is a ray of hope. We can experience life optimistically, expecting a bright future. It is God's desire that we live life abundantly.

I hope this volume will provide some possible answers for life's worries, and enable you to experience a life worth living!

Richard Daly

Hope in God's promises

We could never keep every promise we've ever made. But God is 100 per cent faithful. Every one of God's promises is 'yes' in Christ.

For Further Reflection
2 Corinthians 1:20

Hope on

Hope means hoping even when things
seem hopeless.

Value what you have

Never take a simple breath for granted.
It's a privilege to be alive. In spite of all
cruelty and unfairness, life is beautiful,
precious and an incredible gift. Let us
make the best of it.

For Further Reflection
Psalm 8:3–6

New dawn, new hope

Hope forever tells us that
tomorrow will be better.

For Further Reflection

Lamentations 3:22–23

When all else fails, try Jesus

If you have been reduced to God as your only hope, you're in a good place.

For Further Reflection

Psalm 3:3

Psalm 39:7

Be hopeful in hopelessness

As long as matters seem hopeful, hope remains merely superficial. It's only when everything is hopeless, that hope truly proves its strength.

For Further Reflection

Romans 8:24

Job 5:9

Find hope within

'Life treasures are not far afield upon some distant shore. Jewels of peace and happiness are found right at your door.'

Author unknown

For Further Reflection

Genesis 28:15

Persevere

There are many lessons that can be learnt
from watching children learn to walk.
Countless times they fall, cry and are hurt,
but still get back up and try again. It's a sure
reminder that what we want to accomplish
may not always be easy. But persevere!

For Further Reflection

Matthew 24:13
Matthew 19:14

Let God lead

When the way forward seems a bit blurred, it can be God's way of getting you to recognise that things are changing. That's the time to consult him as to your next move.

For Further Reflection

Proverbs 3:5,6
Psalm 25:5

Explore the qualities of hope

Three relatives of hope:

Willingness – to accept whatever comes knowing you'll come through stronger.
Determination – the ability to stand firm while those around you are falling.
Insight – to see the character-developing hand of God in it all.

With these qualities, you will survive!

For Further Reflection
Romans 5:3–4

Don't settle for second best

Your biggest enemy is not the challenges you face; it's compliancy, negativity, self-imposed limitations and self-pity. The Apostle Paul wrote 'I can do all things through Christ who strengthens me'. That means you can rise above circumstances, if you want to.

For Further Reflection

Philippians 4:13
Proverbs 13:12

Be an encourager

The world is full of discouragers – what
we need is more encouragers. Many times
a word of praise, thanks or appreciation
has kept a person on their feet. Encourage
someone today: it will bring healing.

For Further Reflection

Proverbs 15:23
Isaiah 52:7

Prayer changes things

When a believing person prays, great things happen. When God prompts you to pray for somebody, don't wait to do it! Your prayer may be the only thing standing between that person and catastrophe.

For Further Reflection

James 5:16

Be not dismayed

Remember, life will go on, even if it doesn't go according to your plan. Don't wait until you lose a loved one or have a heart attack before you discover that. Your worth comes from God, his opinion of you never changes.

For Further Reflection
Philippians 4:6

Give thanks every day

Finding time to pray every day will always
be a challenge, because prayer is a learnt
behaviour. So, when you wake up, say,
'Lord, thank you for giving me this new day.
Help me to rejoice and be glad in it.'

For Further Reflection

Psalm 100
Psalm 118:24

Take God at his word

In life people will seek to offend you, for whatever reason. What's important is not what others say about you, it's what you say to yourself. Affirm yourself by the truth of God's word.

For Further Reflection
Psalm 139:16–18

Live to your potential

You can never really tell what potential lies
within, until you have a purpose and a will
to achieve a goal. Life is an adventure;
we get out of it what we put into it.

For Further Reflection
John 10:10

Laughter is the best medicine

It's a fact: laughter increases immunity, and benefits cardiovascular, respiratory, digestive and muscular systems. It reduces pain and stress, increases energy and gives you a sense of wellbeing. It's also contagious!

For Further Reflection

Proverbs 17:22
Ecclesiastes 3:4

Be patient in tribulation

Happiness would not be fully appreciated without an experience of its opposite, sadness. Consider those who have experienced such adversity and learn from them.

For Further Reflection

Romans 12:12

Think happy thoughts

Happiness is a product of attitude and thought. It comes from you, not to you. To be happy, you must think happy.

For Further Reflection

Psalm 128:2

Look for open doors

When one door closes,
God always opens another.

Dispel your fears

The one great enemy of the human race is
fear. The less fear you have, the more health
and harmony you will have. Remember fear
is a bluffer, it boasts more than what it can
really do. Call its bluff, and it will disappear.

For Further Reflection
Isaiah 41:10–14

Hold on

One of the most common mistakes is
thinking that success in life comes from
some magical formula which we do not
possess. Success is simply holding on
and not letting go.

For Further Reflection

Revelation 3:11

Do something creative

Develop a hobby. Do something for the sheer
joy of it. Those who develop a creative and
absorbing interest are better able to stand
up to the stresses and strains of life.

For Further Reflection
Colossians 3:23

Work through your problems

Don't run away from a problem, face it.
Chisel it into small parts, and deal with
each part separately.

For Further Reflection

Matthew 11:28,29
Psalm 55:22

Reminisce to rejuvenate

What are your happiest moments? Savour
again an event of past years, or a long ago
thrill and some of the original warmth of the
occasion will return to cheer the present.

For Further Reflection

Deuteronomy 32:7
Proverbs 10:7

There's power in prayer

Why pray? Because nothing lies beyond the reach of prayer. You'll never know how many people have been strengthened because you asked God to encourage them.

For Further Reflection
James 5:16

Develop an attitude of gratitude

Though your present situation may seem dismal, develop an attitude of gratitude. It's surprising how just giving thanks in all circumstances puts your life into perspective.

For Further Reflection

1 Thessalonians 5:18

The blessed hope

The greatest hope you can ever have as a follower of Christ is the blessed hope of the glorious return of Jesus Christ our Lord.

For Further Reflection

Titus 3:6–7

John 14:1–3

Soul food

There is a common saying, 'you are what you eat'. In other words, to achieve good health we need a balanced diet. Likewise, reading the Bible gives spiritual food for our souls.

For Further Reflection

Deuteronomy 8:3

Trust God's timing

When God plants a dream in your heart,
he starts preparing you for its fulfilment.
He strengthens your character and deepens
your spiritual roots. Don't try to bring it to
birth prematurely, instead trust God's timing.

For Further Reflection

John 12:24

Just for today

This day will only come once. Challenge
yourself by saying, 'Just for today I will enjoy
each moment to the fullest, and try not
to tackle all life's problems at once.
Just for today I will try to enjoy every
one of God's blessings.'

For Further Reflection

Psalm 118:24

Consider your value

Do you realise that when you put yourself
down, you're insulting your maker? God says
you are fearfully and wonderfully made:
in his eyes you are just right.

For Further Reflection
Psalm 139:14
Ephesians 1:11

Trust God

There is only one person who is ultimately
faithful, reliable and dependable and in whom
we can fully trust. As the Scriptures declare,
'Put not your hope in man in whom there
is no hope, but put your hope in God.'

For Further Reflection

Psalm 146:3
Lamentations 3:24

Hold on

When it seems that your prayers are not
being answered, it may be that God is simply
saying 'hold on'. During this time he will
be healing your past so it cannot pollute
your future.

For Further Reflection

Isaiah 49:8

Nothing is too hard for God

Nothing shocks God, or catches him off guard. When the crisis you're facing makes you want to throw in the towel, remember your problems are his opportunities.

For Further Reflection

Matthew 19:26

Mark 14:36

Let it go

The word 'forgive' literally means 'to give
away': it has very little to do with the other
person; it's a decision you make, like exhaling
carbon dioxide from your body because you
know holding on to it will only harm you.
So go ahead, exhale: release forgiveness.

For Further Reflection
Matthew 6:12–15

Start today

The first step to pursuing joy is simply to
begin. The Psalmist says, 'This is the day
that the Lord has made; let us rejoice and
be glad in it.' If we wait until conditions
are perfect, it will never happen.

For Further Reflection

Psalm 118:24
Psalm 68:3

How precious you are

The fact that God cares for you may be hard
to hold on to when you are having a bad day;
but to be cared for means to be wanted, and
despite your failures, God still wants you. It's a
truth that will never go away, so accept it!

For Further Reflection

John 15:15

Learn to relax

Hope fades when we constantly get uptight
about everything: being five minutes
late, getting stuck in traffic, waiting in
line, overcooking a meal, gaining weight,
discovering another grey hair. Lighten up –
release the tension and let hope soar.

For Further Reflection

Romans 5:5
Ecclesiastes 3:12,13

Get staying power

In times of powerlessness it's comforting
to know that God gives power to the weak,
and to those who have no might,
he increases strength.

For Further Reflection
Isaiah 40:29
Isaiah 61:1

More hope, less worry

The Bible says, 'The Lord is faithful, he will guard you from evil.' You may not know what you're being protected from, but God knows: he saves your life every day! So trust him more, complain less; hope in him more, and worry less.

For Further Reflection

2 Thessalonians 3:3
Psalm 103:4

Capture negative thoughts

Low self-esteem arises when we listen to lies
about ourselves. When a negative thought
enters your mind that could be crippling to
your character, capture it, assess it, measure
it up to what God thinks of you, and if it
doesn't match up, throw it out!

For Further Reflection

2 Corinthians 10:5
Philippians 4:7

Put your faith to the test

When you are overwhelmed, it is easy to jump to the conclusion that God isn't on the job. When you can't figure it out, you have to faith it out!

For Further Reflection

Psalm 9:10–11

Use what you've got

It's easy to use our limitations as an excuse
for doing nothing productive with our lives.
But God wants you to develop your strengths
and fulfil your life's purpose. So instead
of dwelling on what you don't have, start
using what you have.

For Further Reflection

Ephesians 2:10

Take God at his word

God has given us his 'promise and his oath'
so in prayer, even though you may not get
the answer you want, you can rest assured he
makes 'everything work together for good'.

For Further Reflection

Hebrews 6:18
Romans 8:28

Appreciate yourself

Everything God made was very good; that
means you, too. Endeavour to see yourself
as God sees you: he wants to change
your self-image so you can appreciate
your unique gifts and qualities.

For Further Reflection
Genesis 1:31

Cherish what's yours

Learning to be content with what we have
puts what we hope for in perspective.
The last commandment says 'do not covet'.
Once we're satisfied with what we've got,
our hopes will not be covetous.

For Further Reflection

Philippians 4:11
1 Timothy 6:8

Enjoy the moment

When you appreciate the moment, you
instinctively know that as long as you have
life, you have hope. Enjoy the moment.

For Further Reflection

Deuteronomy 4:4
Luke 19:9

Choose to be happy

Happiness is not something you pursue;
indeed the more you pursue it, the more
elusive it becomes. Happiness is something
you can choose to accept right now.

For Further Reflection

Psalm 128:2
Acts 26:2

Be optimistic about life

One of the discoveries of modern medicine
is that the more optimistic you are, the
greater your chances of maintaining health.
Simply believe that you will be well:
you've got nothing to lose.

For Further Reflection

Isaiah 65:18
Luke 6:23
James 5:13

Put hope into action

Some conclude that hope is merely an expectation of certain outcomes. It's more than this: hope is a real commitment to positive behaviour and attitudes. It's an active, positive word. Adapt this approach and live an abundant life.

For Further Reflection

Romans 15:13
Romans 12:12

Be calm

A calm state of mind is naturally
accompanied by hope and optimism.
Maintain the calm, and you maintain
the hope.

For Further Reflection

John 14:27
Romans 15:13

Get excited about something

Enthusiasm. What a wonderful action word!
It is an effective, contagious force. It helps
you achieve the impossible and makes the
future full of promise. Be enthusiastic!

For Further Reflection

Psalm 32:11

Psalm 47:1

Give, and it will come back to you

When you go out of your way to do good
for others you derive a double benefit. First,
any selfless act generates a feeling of
well-being, and second, your outlook on
life becomes more meaningful.

For Further Reflection

Luke 6:38
2 Corinthians 9:6–8

Celebrate life

Your birthday is a wonderful opportunity to celebrate the miraculous achievement of what your life has been to date. If there's one thing that's worth celebrating, it's the fact that you are alive.

For Further Reflection

Luke 12:23
John 10:10

Make up your mind

Abraham Lincoln said, 'A man is as happy
as he makes up his mind to be.' The same
can be said of hope: you're as hopeful as
you make up your mind to be.

For Further Reflection
Psalm 45:2
Psalm 71:5,14

Go back to the future

Generally, the problems of today become less threatening with the course of time. If you imagine yourself at some time in the future looking back on your worries today, you'll discover they were not worth worrying about at all.

For Further Reflection

Matthew 6:25–34

Be the change

Gandhi once said, 'Be the change you want to see in the world.' There's no better place to begin than with yourself.

For Further Reflection

Psalm 51:10

Treasure your treasured moments

When you have an inspiring thought or experience, keep a journal to treasure these moments. Over a period of time you will build a collection of your own personal inspirations to refer to in times of need.

For Further Reflection

Isaiah 30:8
Jeremiah 30:2
Revelation 1:19

Keep on keeping on

There is one trait that produces more positive results than knowledge, wealth or fame – persistence. If you just keep going, maintaining your hope and belief that something good will happen, eventually it will.

For Further Reflection
2 Timothy 4:5

Change your ways

It's never too late to change bad habits,
unhelpful patterns of behaviour, fixed
routines, or mundane cycles. All it takes is
commitment, and a change of perspective,
and you can alter the negative.

For Further Reflection
Philippians 3:21

Look forward with hope

No matter how dark and dreary the days
ahead may seem, there is always something
positive to look forward to that can become
your beam of light. Just flick on the switch.

For Further Reflection

Hebrews 12:2

Don't stay down

Life is all about learning from our mistakes;
and the beauty of it is that no matter how
many times we fail, there's always another
chance. Failure is not the falling down;
it's the staying down.

For Further Reflection

Psalm 37:24

Don't be miserable

Miserable people get the same number
of opportunities as happy people. They just
tend to overlook them. Look for the good
and you'll feel much more hopeful.

For Further Reflection
Isaiah 45:22

Keep fit, feel good

As we know, exercise brings our body to
an overall state of good health. It also has
benefits spiritually. By giving us a vitality for
life, exercise gives us a more hopeful outlook.
Isn't that worth working up a sweat for?

For Further Reflection

3 John 2

Turn to the sun

Let the rays of the sun permeate your soul.
Sunlight, apart from being a good source
of vitamin D, staves off those melancholy
moments, and injects hopefulness and
vibrancy into your day.

For Further Reflection
Matthew 13:43

You are what you think

The words you use, like your thoughts, have
a powerful influence on how you behave.
Reinforce your positive behaviour by telling
yourself, 'there is much to live for',
'life does get better', 'there is hope'.

For Further Reflection

Proverbs 23:7

You are indispensable

Remember, you are unique. There is no one else on this planet like you. You are one of a kind, just as important as anyone else in this world, and the contribution you make is vital. So take your rightful place on the podium.

For Further Reflection
Isaiah 43:2

Sow a little hope

The growth cycle of a plant reassures us
of the continuity of life. Germination, the
sprouting plant, its growth and its eventual
natural recycling, all show us that there
is order and purpose in life.

For Further Reflection

Psalm 126:6

Endure your test

What may seem to you to be bitter trials are often blessings in disguise. Take comfort in the hope that when you come through, you will be stronger, as gold tried in the fire.

For Further Reflection
1 Peter 1:7

Relax your face and smile

Smiling relaxes your face. You use less facial muscles than when frowning and communicate good feelings toward others and within yourself.

For Further Reflection

Proverbs 15:13
Nehemiah 2:2

Keep focused

When you have a purpose in life, you will be less affected by the obstacles that come in your way. Instead of seeing them as hindrances, they become stepping stones to success.

For Further Reflection
Philippians 3:13,14

Release your potential

Every new opportunity in life remains only
potential until you take that first step forward.
Go forward, take the first step, and the rest
of the journey will take care of itself.

For Further Reflection

Psalm 16:11
Psalm 119:105

The serenity of prayer

'God grant me the courage to change
the things I can, the patience to accept
the things I can't, and the wisdom to
know the difference.'

For Further Reflection

James 1:5

It gets easier

It's always the beginning of a task that seems the most challenging – riding a bike, playing the piano, learning a language. It's most difficult just before it starts to get easier. So take courage: when it seems daunting, your life could be about to turn for the better.

For Further Reflection

2 Timothy 2:3
Matthew 24:13

War of the mind

You can think yourself into happiness or success, despair or hopefulness. It all depends how you manage the volume of one type of thought over the other. The one that dominates the mind tends to be the winner. The good thing is that you decide who will win.

For Further Reflection

Isaiah 26:3
Luke 12:29

Look up

It's only when we walk with our head down
that we bump into lamp posts – with our
chin up and head straight, in the dark the
same lamp post becomes our light and guide.

For Further Reflection

Micah 7:7

It's worth the wait

On earth we have the pain without the reason. In heaven we have the reason without the pain.

For Further Reflection
Revelation 21:4

Go forward

There are many things in life that we have
no control over, especially things in the past.
Acknowledging these areas in life will
enable us to move forward and create
new pathways for the future.

For Further Reflection

Isaiah 38:17
Philippians 3:13

Don't worry

The things we worry about rarely become a
reality. It's like dynamite without a flame to
light it, potentially destructive but actually
powerless. In fact, the only damage it does
is rob you of a hopeful tomorrow.

For Further Reflection
Philippians 4:6

Think ahead

You limit your future when you dwell in the past. You can accomplish a lot more by envisioning your future plans. Actualise it in your mind, see it before it happens.

For Further Reflection

Proverbs 23:4

Treat others well

'Do unto others as you would have them
do unto you.' The golden rule, if practised,
can lead to a golden experience.

For Further Reflection
Micah 12:33
Leviticus 19:18

Take nothing for granted

When you lower your assumptions of what
you expect from other people, you will
receive a welcome surprise. Assume nothing,
but know that great things lie ahead for you.

For Further Reflection
Philippians 2:3

Lessons from a baby

The birth of a baby is the personification of hope. It ought to remind you not only of a perfect creator, but also a perfect sustainer of life.

For Further Reflection

Ecclesiastes 9:4
Romans 8:24

Choose a positive ring tone

Choose a ring tone that instils positive thoughts every time it rings. Not only will you not mind the phone ringing, but the words will reinforce feelings of well being. How about 'I Feel Good' by James Brown!

For Further Reflection

2 Chronicles 7:6

1 Samuel 16:23

Look for the good

Despite our faults or failings, we all have
something positive that's worthwhile.
To discover it in those around you, just
look for it – but be aware, it may mean
choosing to ignore the negative.

For Further Reflection

Proverbs 12:25, 15:23
1 Thessalonians 5:21

Show genuine love

Amid so many rules and laws, we're told to abide by two commands: 'Love your God with all your heart', and 'Love your fellow men'. If we truly practise this, everything else will fall into place.

For Further Reflection
Mark 12:28–33

Act what you believe

When you act as though life has something
special in store for you, you'll soon discover
it's true. Not only is it a biblical promise, but
you also convince your subconscious, and
this becomes self-fulfilling.

For Further Reflection
Mark 9:23

'Big up' yourself

If no one else is around to compliment you,
go ahead and do it yourself. Congratulate
and reassure yourself. If there's one person
it pays to have on your side, it's you!

For Further Reflection
Psalm 139:14

Maintain your friendships

An important factor in inspiring you to be hopeful is the support of old friends. Treasure those associations – it's so easy to be 'out of sight, out of mind'. If you have an old friend, don't let them go.

For Further Reflection
Proverbs 17:17

Don't neglect God's leading

Sometimes we forget the struggles we've been through and how God helped us get through them. Take time out today and reflect on how God has helped you in the past. It will give you added confidence for the future.

For Further Reflection
Isaiah 46:9

All things bright and beautiful

If you want to inject feelings of brightness
and jubilance, surround yourself with
colourful flowers. The fragrance alone
acts as a healing balm.

For Further Reflection
Isaiah 40:6

Maintain your integrity

The satisfaction of a job well done will bring
rewards of its own. If you work diligently and
faithfully, you not only feel a greater sense of
achievement, but contentment that you've
done your best, even if no one else notices.

For Further Reflection

Proverbs 13:11

Read more, watch less

Usually your imagination is more active
when you're reading than when you're
watching. That's why literature can have a
more uplifting and long-lasting effect than
more passive mediums of entertainment.
Spend time reading books, and let your
imagination work.

For Further Reflection

2 Timothy 2:15

A prayer of hope

Thank you Lord for filling my past and my
present with your love, your mercy and your
grace. Thank you for the promise that I can
spend all my tomorrows with you.

For Further Reflection
Hebrews 6:19

A poem of hope

'Be content, my heart, though you cannot
see God's vast eternal mystery. Be at peace,
my soul, like a child at rest, in the simple
truth that God knows best.'

For Further Reflection
2 Corinthians 4:16–18

A time to dance

The wise king Solomon said, 'for everything
there is a season', and goes on to list
many events in life. When you've cried all
your tears, dance. You'll be surprised
how therapeutic it can be.

For Further Reflection
2 Samuel 6:14
Psalm 30:11

Hope in God

Remember, God is not bound by our circumstances, neither is he overcome by our turmoil. In every situation he has power to provide a way out for you. Put your hope in him.

For Further Reflection
Psalm 121:1–3

The hope of the world

'Life with Christ is an endless hope,
without him a hopeless end.'

Anonymous

For Further Reflection
Philippians 1:20,21

Look up

When looking backward is filled with pain
and looking forward seems ominous;
try looking upward.

For Further Reflection
Psalm 107:28–30

Hold on to hope

'Today well-lived makes every tomorrow
a vision of hope.'

Anonymous

For Further Reflection
Romans 15:13

Hope in the future

As a believer in God you can confidently say,
'Although I don't know what the future holds,
I know who holds the future!'

For Further Reflection
Deuteronomy 1:29–30

Be proactive

Don't wait for the opportunities to do good,
make the opportunities.

For Further Reflection

Colossians 1:10
Proverbs 12:25

You're never alone

When you're alone, you can be certain of
one thing: even though you may not feel his
presence, God is with you – he will never
fail in his promises.

For Further Reflection

Joshua 1:5,6

A beacon of hope

'The world cries out with a common voice,
"Is there hope? Where can hope be?" To our
wounded world God still replies, "With the
cross of Calvary".'

B.J. Huff

For Further Reflection
Isaiah 55:3

Decide on your own ending

Do not think of your problems as a full stop, but merely as a comma. You can decide how the rest of the sentence will run.

For Further Reflection

Philippians 1:6

Let hope heal

In times of illness, the human body experiences a natural gravitational pull in the direction of hope. That's why the patient's hope is the physician's secret weapon. It is the hidden ingredient in any prescription.

For Further Reflection

Jeremiah 17:14

Cast your cares on him

At the cross, Jesus took on all our sins and
troubles and placed them on himself. Yet the
sacrifice wasn't just a one-off, he is more than
willing to do it for you again and again.
What sacrificial love!

For Further Reflection

Romans 5:8

Fear not

The fear of what might happen tomorrow
is far worse than the actual experience
of any present sorrow. Don't take upon
yourself unnecessary pain. Ask God
to banish the fears.

For Further Reflection
Lamentations 3:57,58

Focus on the little things

It is the little things that usually have the
greatest impact in life – a compliment, a
smile, a thank you, a hug. It's these things
that make up a positive outlook.

Never give in

'Never give in, never give in. Never, never, never, never – in nothing, great or small, large or petty, never give in, except to convictions of honour and good sense.'

Winston Churchill

For Further Reflection

Jeremiah 7:24
1 Thessalonians 5:21

Start afresh

'Today is the first day of the rest of your life.'

Dale Carnegie

For Further Reflection

Proverbs 4:18
Psalm 118:24

Hope is life

'What oxygen is to the lungs, such is hope
to the meaning of life.'

Emil Brumes

For Further Reflection
1 Timothy 4:9–10

Act on inspiration

It's not inspiring books or presentations that change people's lives; they simply act as a catalyst. It is what you choose to believe and act upon, that's where the change comes. No one can change the life of any individual except that individual.

For Further Reflection

Joshua 24:15

Claim the gift

'Yesterday's history,
Tomorrow's a mystery.
All we have is Today, and it's
called the present
Because it's a precious gift.'

Anonymous

For Further Reflection

James 1:17

Metamorphosis

What the caterpillar sees as the end,
the butterfly sees as just the beginning.
It's the same life with a new outfit.

_____

For Further Reflection
2 Corinthians 5:17

You are who you are

When you start comparing yourself with others, eventually you will become either resentful or vain, for there will always be greater or lesser people than you. Be yourself. Accept yourself. Appreciate yourself!

For Further Reflection

1 Peter 2:9

Attitude problems

Your attitude dictates your whole approach
to life. The good news is, you can alter your
life simply by changing your attitude.

For Further Reflection

Psalm 37:5

Trust yourself

Intuition is the ability to discern based on
instinct. To many questions of your life, the
answers really lie within. Instead of constantly
listening to others – listen to yourself.
You are your own solution.

For Further Reflection
Isaiah 30:21

Get up again

Falling down is a temporary condition.
Staying down is what makes it permanent.

For Further Reflection

Isaiah 37:24
Micah 7:8

Don't let go

'When you get to the end of the rope,
tie a knot and hold on.'

Franklin D. Roosevelt

For Further Reflection

1 Thessalonians 5:21

Flee temptation

We are promised that in every tempting
situation, there is always a way of escape.
Don't get caught, look for the exit.

For Further Reflection

1 Corinthians 10:13
Revelation 3:10

Here today, gone tomorrow

'And it came to pass', is a common phrase
in the Old Testament. It is a reminder that,
whatever our present turmoil – be hopeful,
it too will pass.

For Further Reflection
2 Samuel 11:1,2
Romans 8:18

Believe, and you will

If you believe you can, you can.
If you believe you can't, you can't.
So what do you want to believe?

For Further Reflection

Mark 11:24
Mark 9:23

Leave it to God

'If we have faith the size of a mustard seed,
we can move mountains.' Don't look at the
mountain, look to the mountain mover.

For Further Reflection

Matthew 17:20
Matthew 21:21

Daily guidance

'Lord, let me live one day at a time.
My choice determined by your will,
My path illumined by light,
My faith grounded in your truth,
My heart set on eternity.'

For Further Reflection

Proverbs 4:11

Expect the unexpected

If you travel a path in life without obstacles, you're probably going around in circles. The only guaranteed thing in life is its unexpectednesses.

For Further Reflection

John 16:33

Do it even when afraid

Facing our fears is sometimes the hardest thing to do. Not everything that is faced can be changed, but nothing can be changed unless it is faced.

For Further Reflection

Isaiah 41:10

Exodus 14:13

Try nothing, gain nothing

What would you attempt to do if you knew
you would fail? What would you lose
if you never attempted? In every attempt
there's always a lesson.

For Further Reflection

1 Samuel 17:32
Luke 22:33

Count your blessings

The words of the hymn writer still ring true, 'Count your blessings, name them one by one ... and it will surprise you what the Lord has done'. That's one hymn worth putting into practice!

For Further Reflection

Ephesians 1:3
Malachi 3:10

Learn your lessons

When you've come through your test in life,
commune with God to discover what
lesson he would have you learn.

For Further Reflection

Psalm 25:4

Turn a minus to plus

Find courage in dis-courage-ment.
An appointment in dis-appointments
and hope in hope-lessness.

For Further Reflection

Job 41:22
Psalm 30:11

Be patient

Whether it's the best of times or the worst of times, remember there are other times to come.

For Further Reflection
Psalm 30:5

Look to the cross

We all have our crosses to bear, some large, some small, but because of the cross Christ carried, we all have the hope of eternal life.

For Further Reflection
1 John 2:25

Turn it over to Jesus

We are invited to 'cast our burdens on the
Lord', with the promise, 'he will sustain you.'
The emphasis is on 'sustain' – that means to
strengthen and nourish you throughout.

For Further Reflection

Psalm 55:22
1 Peter 5:7

Keep going

If you're going through hell –
don't stop, keep going!

Wait for the morning

The Psalmist provides this wonderful verse:
'Weeping may endure for the night, but joy
comes in the morning.'

For Further Reflection
Psalm 30:5

Head for the stars

'Two men looked out of prison bars,
one saw mud, the other saw stars.'

For Further Reflection

Deuteronomy 4:19
Psalm 121:1

You have an invisible friend

Unseen by us, within the spiritual realm
at any time needed, God sends his angels
of hope to bring us invincible help.
You are not alone.

For Further Reflection

Psalm 91:11
Psalm 34:7

Footprints in the sand

When you think your prayers are not being answered and you see only one set of footprints in the sand, be assured they're not yours – God is carrying you, and your load.

For Further Reflection

Isaiah 53:4

God is omnipresent

Since Jesus Christ is 'the same yesterday,
today and forever', we can take the Christ
of yesterday; walk with him today, and ask
him to guide our paths for tomorrow –
for he's already there.

For Further Reflection

Hebrews 13:8
Psalm 139:7

God has a plan for you

'For I know the thoughts I think towards you,'
says the Lord, 'thoughts of peace and not of
evil, to give you a future and a hope.'

For Further Reflection

Jeremiah 29:11

Lean on God

To put your faith in God is to lean your whole weight upon him. It also means removing the crutch.

For Further Reflection

Proverbs 3:4,5

Good things come to those who wait

'Those who wait on the Lord shall renew their strength; they shall mount up with wings like eagles. They shall run and not be weary, they shall walk and not faint.'

For Further Reflection

Isaiah 40:37

Let God work it out

Leaving the details of your future in
God's hands is the most responsible act
of obedience you can make. It's also
the ultimate act of faith.

For Further Reflection

Romans 8:28

Be Spirit-led

'Trust in the Lord with all your heart and
lean not on your own understanding;
in all your ways acknowledge him and
he shall direct your paths.'

For Further Reflection

Proverbs 3:5–6

Avoid a quick fix

When we present our problems to God
he doesn't give temporary relief,
he offers a permanent solution.

For Further Reflection

2 Thessalonians 2:16
Isaiah 26:4
Isaiah 60:19,20

Saved by grace

'Amazing grace, how sweet the sound
that saved a wretch like me,
I once was lost but now am found
Was blind but now I see.'

John Newton

For Further Reflection
Ephesians 2:5,8

Hope changes the world

'Everything that is done in the world
is done by hope.'

Martin Luther King

For Further Reflection

Ecclesiastes 9:4
Romans 8:24

Cherish your experiences

Experience comes by persevering through life's encounters. It is a valuable asset. Every addition to it enhances your life.

For Further Reflection

James 1:2

Look to the light

No one ever damaged their eyesight
by looking on the brighter side of life.

For Further Reflection

2 Corinthians 4:18
Isaiah 45:22

Submit to God

When we fully surrender to Christ, we begin to look at life through his eyes, and we learn to face the future through his strength.

For Further Reflection

James 4:7

Be a comforter

When God comforts us it's not necessarily
to make us comfortable, but, once comforted,
to then go on and be a comforter to others.

For Further Reflection
2 Corinthians 1:3–5

Let God mould you

As the potter is to the clay, so God is to our lives. However you might presently feel, remember, God has not finished with you yet.

_____

For Further Reflection

Jeremiah 18:6

Experience a new life

Conversion is a wonderful spiritual term.
It means rebirth – a new life. It is the ultimate
source of hope for the person who wants
a change in their life.

For Further Reflection
Luke 22:32
John 3:6